POCKET BOOK *of Hope*

WORDS OF INSPIRATION

NOVALIS

bayard

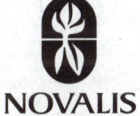

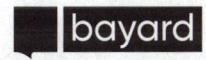

❡Living with Chriſt

© 2024 Novalis Publishing Inc.

Cover design and layout:
Audrey Wells

Cover images: Dove: iStock Photo/bubaone; green background: iStock Photo/ShutterWorx

Interior images: Dreamstime

Published in Canada by Novalis

Publishing Office
1 Eglinton Avenue East
Suite 800
Toronto, Ontario, Canada
M4P 3A1

Head Office
4475 Frontenac Street
Montréal, Québec, Canada
H2H 2S2

en.novalis.ca

Cataloguing in Publication is available from Library and Archives Canada

ISBN: 978-2-89830-181-0

We acknowledge the support of the Government of Canada.

5 4 3 2 1

Published in the United States by Bayard, Inc.

Publishing Office:
Bayard, Inc.
500 Salisbury St.
Worcester, MA 01698
tel: 1-800-321-0411
www.livingwithchrist.us

ISBN: 978-1-62785-829-8

NOVALIS

bayard

Printed in Canada.

All rights reserved. No part of this publication may be reproduced, stored in a retrieval system, or transmitted in any form, or by any means, electronic, mechanical, photocopying, recording, or otherwise, without the written permission of the publisher.

28 27 26 25 24

Contents

Introduction, by Anne Louise Mahoney 5

Hope Takes Care, by Greg Kennedy 9

The Best Is Yet to Be, by Catherine Mulroney 16

Hope from the Prophets of Today, by Glen Argan 22

A Promise of What Can Be, by Mariette Martineau 28

God Holds Death and Life, by Donald Bolen 34

An Unwavering Spark, by Stefany Dupont 40

Storying Our Hope, by Stephen Bede Scharper 45

Sustaining Sources of Hope, by Christine Way Skinner 54

The Hand of God, by Constance Price 61

Social Movements, Fountains of Social Hope,
  by Joe Gunn 67

"That's Why You Were Baptized": The Decision
  to Hope, by Anne Walsh 74

Introduction
Hope Does Not Disappoint Us

When Pope Francis declared that 2025 would be a Jubilee year with the theme "Pilgrims of Hope," he got me thinking about what hope is. It's much more than wishful thinking. It's even more than optimism or seeing what might be possible. Ultimately, it's about nourishing a tiny flame, trusting that the fire will not be extinguished. We keep hope alive by feeding it, tending it, sharing it. For if we're called to be pilgrims of hope, then it's a path we walk together.

Saint Paul knew a thing or two about hope. His words continue to inspire us and spur us on, even during dark times:

> We also boast in our sufferings, knowing that suffering produces endurance, and endurance produces character, and character produces hope, and hope does not disappoint us, because God's love has been poured into our hearts through the Holy Spirit that has been given to us. (Romans 5:1-5)

Saint Augustine (354–430) put it another way: "Hope has two beautiful daughters; their names are Anger and Courage. Anger at the way things are, and Courage to see that they do not remain as they are."

Hope, then, is not a passive thing. It could be one of the greatest actions of our lives! When we can look beyond our current reality – from conflict to poverty to injustice to climate change – we will discover the actions we need to take to get us, and our fellow pilgrims, through to the other side. No one says this will be easy, but our faith can support us, and we can support each other.

Psychologists talk about "glimmers" – little ordinary moments in the day that bring us peace, joy or gratitude. By opening our eyes to the glimmers around us, we build up our sense that the world is a place where good things happen, which can help us when bad things also inevitably happen. Glimmers feed our sense of hope.

In this *Pocket Book of Hope*, writers from various disciplines and walks of life share what gives them hope in times of trouble, loss or pain. At the heart of their reflections is Christian hope in God's love and God's

goodness – the deep knowledge that God is with us always and that new life always springs from moments of death and destruction.

As we nurture the flame in our own lives, we also find the strength to share it with others whose flame has dwindled or gone out. As the glow spreads from person to person, we light the way on our pilgrimage of hope.

Anne Louise Mahoney is the editor of Looking to the Laity: Reflections on Where the Church Can Go from Here *and of* Neverending Love: Sharing Stories, Prayers and Comfort for Miscarriage and Infant Loss, *and is the author of* I Hope, *a book for young children.*

Hope Takes Care

GREG KENNEDY

Hope sent me ahead to say
she'll be late
but don't worry
we can start without her.

EVERYBODY IS WRITING about hope these days. This proliferation could result from various factors. Is there so much hope around that all our words about it simply arise from observing its abundance? We mention the Olympic Games, for example, much more frequently every four years. Or has a general scarcity made us anxious to manufacture more so that we're doing our best to communicate hope into existence?

Environmentalists, having learned that a steady diet of doom leads to overweight despair out of shape for positive action, now spice their bad news with reasons for "determined optimism." Fear, they've discovered, makes for a pretty shoddy motivator over the long haul, especially when the threats are not immediately perceptible and the sacrifices required are sustained.

If the whole bloody mess looks fated to failure, then only the foolhardy put in the effort to clean up. On the other hand, even a small glimmer of hope can draw action out of wills that otherwise would languish in depressed darkness.

Sufficiently aware of the alarming science and the sobering histories of former civilizations that outstripped the carrying capacity of their habitats, I am quite certain that the future of many will be as grim and unforgiving as the tragic present is for a growing number of people. In actual numbers, no other period in the past has witnessed the level of forced migration of people fleeing drought, violence, famine, flooding, etc., all caused or at the very least exacerbated by climate change. Our objectification of the animate world, toughened by the abuses that inevitably follow from this desecration, have driven us to the brink of massive death and suffering. It used to break my heart. Now I mostly shake my head. Sometimes I pinch myself to make sure I still feel and haven't fallen into a detached somnambulant stupor.

Yet, at my truest and most contemplative moments, I don't suspect that indifference really has infected my system and deadened my nerve endings. While I know the undertow is pulling us into the choppy deep, my feet still feel a truth at the bottom of the peril. Although ultimately inexpressible, this grounding truth can be pointed at in many ways. Here, the closest statement I can offer is that the Creator will not abandon Creation. In other words, "Be not afraid."

This imperative gets a great deal of airtime in the Bible. While it has universal and eternal application, today, obedience to it is both dangerous and irresponsible if decoupled from its twin command: "Be very careful." To go through climate-changed, sixth-extinction, chemical- and plastic-saturated life unconcerned is less a sign of faith than of insanity. The state of biological health, currently sliding down the scale from riches to rags, deserves our fullest and finest attention. A cavalier nonchalance with (dis)respect to the suffering Creation at best insults, at worst assaults, the Creator. "Be not afraid" cannot mean what's going on is no big deal.

The sanest (not to mention saintliest) response to a collapsing biosphere involves taking extraordinary care. It is also the most hopeful response. Care has a built-in forward perspective. We don't typically take care of garbage because we don't see any future in it.

The very definition of trash could be "stuff that has run its course." We treat such matter with indifference, if not disgust, despite the service it has provided to us. Care, on the contrary, perceives life beyond the apparent "death" of the object used up. Care invests energy into the possibility of change. To this extent, living without fear requires much active care. Without care's hopeful investment in the future, we will always, strain and fight as we may, be afraid.

My hope, it turns out, is tied to my care. This may sound odd. People burdened with cares don't usually come across as all that hopeful. They can give the impression that existence is pure struggle, endurance and unrelenting effort. Such weighty ways of engaging reality threaten to dismantle joy, which surely is an essential element of hope. When does hopeful caring slip into humourless, oppressive cares? It happens when the carer loses sight of the embodied being (person or other creature) in need of succour.

The anointing at Bethany (Mark 14:3-9) provides a striking biblical illustration of this danger. A woman finds Jesus, already in the anxious grip of anticipating his demise, and soothes him with an uncalculated act of love. Some were indignant at the sight of this apparent excess. Why waste such costly perfume? was their complaint. These people, not ill-intentioned but likely fearful, had lost their sense of care that sees into the future. Jesus takes the woman's part. She has prepared my body for what's to come, he tells them. In other words, she has cared for what others will try to destroy. By "wasting" the oil, she has preserved the worth of his flesh, his incarnation, his pertinence to Earth. The body of Jesus will soon be trashed, but the woman somehow saw beyond that hopeless destruction and invested in possibility beyond death. I'd like to think that her care not only prepared the body for burial, but much more for resurrection. She cared so much that her hands rubbed hope into the meaning of his material being.

We are called to do the same. Writing about hope will only get us so far. If we don't start caring for the generous creatures, both animate and inanimate, of this Earth, pouring out our thanks and love on them in ways that could appear excessive, but in fact are restorative and full of promise, we'll lose all hold on hope. It will slip right through our fisted and fearful hands. Hope takes care and care takes hope into new life where it once looked wasted.

*my only hope
these days
is when
it's all over
i take the pains
to press play
again*

Greg Kennedy works as spiritual director and Executive Director at Ignatius Jesuit Centre in Guelph, Ontario. He has authored Reupholstered Psalms *and* Amazing Friendships between Animals and Saints *(Novalis).*

The Best Is Yet to Be

Catherine Mulroney

*Grow old along with me!
The best is yet to be.*

Rabbi Ben Ezra
Robert Browning

Grow old along with Michael. That had always been the plan.

As I looked down the road to retirement, I could imagine only happiness. I was so confident about it that there was no need to hope. I *knew* our best years were coming. After decades of work and a commitment to raising our family, we were now in a position to slow down a bit, enjoy our now grown-up children and really focus on enjoying each other's company. We'd take all those trips we'd dreamed about, and tackle the house projects we kept putting off, and enjoy the passel of grandchildren we were sure we would have someday soon.

Instead, when I was 59, Michael, my husband of 36 years, was diagnosed with cancer. He died within the year, a few weeks after he turned 66 and just days after our youngest turned 25.

The year that Mike was sick was brutal, filled with dread and fear, worry and stress. What I hadn't anticipated, however, was that it was also the moment I finally came to understand the most elemental nature of hope.

Hope is often backlit by confidence and naïveté, directing our thoughts to positive outcomes and to attaining the things we want and think we need. This form of hope is childlike, assuming that, if we close our eyes, clench our fists, and wish *really* hard, only good things will follow. This hope is also often directed toward the trivial. We keep our fingers crossed in hope, wishing for things to be the way we want them to be. And so, we hope for a sunny day for our picnic, or that the car will start on a bitterly cold winter morning. We hope for the best and close the door on any other scenario.

At its core, however, a mature hope is also a form of prayer, a recognition of our own frailty, our very vulnerability. It is an acknowledgement that we have limited control over our lives, and even less over the lives of the people we love. To hope is to acknowledge that things might not always go our way and, when that hope is laid bare, it becomes a desire for reassurance that we can cope with whatever comes our way. Hope, therefore, goes hand in hand with grace.

In the year that Mike was sick, our kids and I hoped liked mad. We hoped for the desired outcomes from all the scans and tests, and we hoped for good news from his appointments every three weeks with his oncologist. We hoped to find ways to brighten his toughest days and we hoped to ease his physical suffering and mental anguish.

And, as death neared, we hoped his suffering would end and that he would find peace.

After Michael died, we learned that hope hadn't disappeared from our lives but had merely shifted. We hoped, for example, that we could offer solace to his grieving co-workers, who deeply felt the loss of a beloved colleague. We also hoped that the donation of his eyes would either improve the life of someone experiencing vision loss or assist in vital ocular research that might someday help someone else.

As a mother, I also had many other hopes. I hoped that my children could find ways to cope with losing their father at too young an age. That they would know that life wasn't over and that it still held out the opportunity of unbelievable happiness and great joy. I hoped they would soon come to see that life would rebuild around that bottomless sorrow and learn that an experience of great loss would heighten the glorious moments in life, as bittersweet as they might be.

I also found I had hopes for myself. Alone for the first time in my life, I hoped I could regroup and find ways to entertain myself and take on all the tasks that once fell into Mike's column. I also hoped that my children wouldn't worry about me. I know they are there if I need them, but they have their own lives to lead. I'll be fine – I hope!

If asked to define my experience of hope today, I'd say it is radically different than when I was younger. Hope no longer rests in promotions and possessions but in the desire to reframe my future. If I am to be on my own, I want to make sure I don't waste my time. I'll confess: it isn't always easy, but I sure am trying to maintain a hopeful view of life. That's what Mike would want.

Often, these days, I find hope in the simplest, most beautiful of moments, whether it's my grandson haul-

ing himself up to a standing position as he teeters on the brink of walking, or my two-year-old granddaughter chattering away to herself about all that fascinates and amuses her. My grandchildren have their whole lives ahead of them, and I hope that their lives are as perfect as they can be.

Ultimately, of course, my heart rests in the great hope of the resurrection. If I can pass on anything to my family, it is the certainty that this life is not the end and that the grief of the cross is defeated by the hope of the stone rolled away.

When I think of Mike now, I feel only gratitude for the life we shared. Of course, we faced challenges but, as he noted on his deathbed, we had a wonderful life. In that gratitude, I am finding something that is pretty new to me: the courage to move forward alone.

And so I do, in hope, putting one foot in front of the other, burning memories into my brain, because there's so much I'll want to update Mike on when I next see him.

After all, the best *is* yet to be.

Author and editor Catherine Mulroney is the mother of four and grandmother of two. She lives in Toronto, where she gardens, reads – and babysits!

Hope from the Prophets of Today

GLEN ARGAN

EARLY ON THE morning of September 17, 1984, the sky was blue, the temperature chilly as people gathered for the papal Mass in a farmer's field north of Edmonton. By the time Mass began, dark clouds were moving in from the northwest and the wind blew hard, knocking over the processional cross which had just been placed in its stand. This was no mere change in the weather: the storm insinuated an imminent apocalypse.

The Gospel that day was the scene from the Last Judgment in Matthew 25, where Christ separated the sheep from the goats. Those who feed the hungry, clothe the naked, visit prisoners and welcome strangers will be invited into God's eternal kingdom. Those indifferent to the needs of others will receive eternal punishment.

In his homily, Pope John Paul II, like a modern Jeremiah, brought the reading into today's world. "In the light of Christ's words, the poor South will judge the rich North," he thundered. "And the poor people and poor nations – poor in different ways, not only lacking food, but also deprived of freedom and other human rights – will judge those people who take these goods away from them, amassing to themselves the imperialistic monopoly of economic and political supremacy at the expense of others."

The force of the pope's prophetic denunciation shook me physically and spiritually. The pope spoke not only of rendering charity to individuals but also of our duty to challenge structures of domination and oppression so justice and peace will prevail.

The eternal fate of each person will be determined by how we treat the poorest and most neglected in our midst. But as did Jesus, Pope John Paul offered promise as well as denunciation. Jesus promises eternal life with him if we see his face in the faces of those who have been cast to the margins of society.

Some would say we ought not to dwell on the negative, that we ought to accentuate the positive in every situation. They maintain that putting a shiny, smiling face on everything is a sign of hope. I disagree. To ignore the reality that we live in dark, dark times is not hope but escapism. Hope can only be born when we see with clear eyes and touch with our own hands the depravity of our world. Isaiah says point blank that those who walk in darkness are the ones who see a great light. To turn our gaze away from suffering and evil is the path to destruction, not hope.

Where can we find hope?

My personal hope is invested neither in technological improvements nor in a future of material prosperity. I draw my hope from sacrificial victims such as Alexei Navalny, Martin Luther King and Mahatma Gandhi. All three were killed because of their prophetic leadership, eschewing violent change but standing four-square against evil. Each had a vision of a world where oppression has ended and where people walk together in harmony.

It was their naming of specific forms of oppression and those who benefited from that oppression which drew the ire of the powerful. When they painted vivid descriptions of a bright future when the mighty would be cast down so the lowly could be raised, they gave hope to the many.

Like Jesus, their prophecy drew the enmity of the powerful, and they gave their lives in pursuit of the beauty of human dignity. Their deaths were not failures but beacons of hope, signs that while the person could be killed, the promise of their lives would only grow brighter.

I am a white, middle-class man in his early 70s. I enjoy excellent health and have a good marriage with four adult children. My life has had a few rough spots but no events that were not overcome with time and grace. Although I am in the latter third of my life, death does not yet press in upon me. Light is stronger than darkness in my life. Given all that, hope would not seem to be the main message I need to hear.

However, all of us live amid a descending gloom. The possibility of a new era of authoritarian political rule is evident. Climate change threatens the stability of every nation's economy and food supply. Civil strife rising out of the vast gap between rich and poor may upend social stability. Runaway inflation may devour a family's life savings. Global war, while perhaps unlikely, is a real prospect.

These are not paranoid delusions but elements of the human condition in the early 21st century. The darkness may swallow the light with little warning. Our comfortable materialism is a mirage.

Hope comes when a voice cries out. The voice lights a flame that all can see amid the darkness. Forces of darkness may extinguish the flame, but once it has been seen, it will not be forgotten. There may be another burst of light. A second light will ignite a third and then a fourth.

They tried to kill Pope John Paul but failed. The torch he ignited in Poland spread rapidly. Within 10 years, the mighty Soviet empire collapsed. The light exposed that the empire was a house of cards. All it needed was a little shove.

Pope John Paul concluded his homily in 1984 with a message of hope: "God, his Spirit, the Holy Spirit, is working in the souls of every one of us, and that is this divine dimension of human existence," he said. Prophets are driven not by anger and despair, but by the Spirit dwelling within.

As the Mass drew to a close on that chilly morning, the dark clouds dissipated and the sun brightened the sky. If we are attuned to Christ, despair will never have the last word. Hidden behind the dark clouds is the promise of a new and radiant day. My hope is rooted in the conviction that God will always carry us through the storm. We should never be afraid.

Glen Argan has been a writer and editor in Canada's Catholic press for more than 45 years. He lives in Edmonton, Alberta.

A Promise of What Can Be

Mariette Martineau

"Can you smell them? The oranges?" In the book *At the Border Called Hope: Where Refugees are Neighbours*, author Mary Jo Leddy refers to the orange trees on the outskirts of Jerusalem. Leddy compares hope to the scent that emanates from the trees in the spring. The oranges were not yet present, but their scent was. There was the "hope" of fruit. Is that what hope is – a promise of what can be? A promise of change? Healing? Safety?

Five years ago, a close friend of mine lost her 21-year-old son to suicide. Her deep pain was raw and real and unfathomable. One path of support I offered to her and the local community was through reflections of hope posted on Facebook. It was like I needed to find a way to proclaim over and over, there is hope… there is hope…

I posted about community and shared grief as hope: "This image surfaced during prayer for me – a woman was standing in her backyard holding a dandelion puff. As I looked closer, the puff's seeds were tiny broken hearts. The woman blew on the puff and the tiny seeds scattered throughout the community. I watched as women of all ages reached up and caught a seed and held it close to their hearts..." Hope is carried by community in times of grief and suffering.

I posted about the tomb: "It feels like an empty tomb kind of day. The skies are weeping, and the birds are chirping as if with some tentative reassurance to one another. The tomb is empty, a tiny step of moving forward is being undertaken, yet not without fear and deep sorrow. Loss will be in our steps for many months to come, yet splashes of light and joy will also sprout up around us as rain does that. 'Peace,' the angel said to the women at the tomb: 'peace.'" Hope is scattered amid the pain – gentle splashes of possible healing.

I posted about darkness and pain and hope: "Sometimes the only place you can be is in the tomb in the darkness. Help is needed to roll away the stone as the heart is stretching its way back to an operational degree of functionality. The pain feels unbearable at times, yet as women we know the pain of labour – at its worst peaks, we can't see beyond it, and all there exists is pain. Until we hear the cry..." A moment makes

all the difference in experiencing hope, one moment amid many moments of pain.

I posted about being holders of hope: "Sometimes we can't find the light, yet others are somehow able to bounce the light onto us or hold it for us until we can hold it for ourselves. It is there and will never stop seeking us. Neither life nor death can separate us from it." In deep experiences of pain, we need people around us to carry hope for us, to reflect it to us in times when we simply cannot grasp it.

I posted about the road to Emmaus: "I find myself pondering two connected realities this morning: the expression 'I am not myself,' spoken to me by a mother in deep grief, and the disciples' inability to recognize Jesus after his resurrection. They had been with him, intensely, for about three and a half years. Jesus walks up to them on the Emmaus road and talks with them and they can't recognize him. Not until he breaks bread with them. So, who wasn't themselves? Scholars will say that Jesus may have been transformed as he was resurrected after all. Yet, I imagine how heavy the hearts were of the disciples, as they had lost both a best friend and a Messiah. In their grief, did they have a sense of not being themselves? Or this intense grief was so hard to navigate that they hadn't 'been themselves' as a grieving person: they just couldn't see him as their 'Jesus radar' was off? Grieving hearts are still our hearts, we are still ourselves, just not maybe who we want to be, just maybe not breathing in the ways we normally do. May our oxygen be filled with a little extra patience for ourselves, with a little more comfort with the pain that is part of our days, with a little more acceptance of 'It's still me, but a me in grief...' The disciples kept walking with this stranger who listened to them in their angst. They did come to and recognize Jesus, and so will we. So will we." Hope is nurtured through ordinary things, familiar tasks, even when we are not ourselves.

I posted about being in a dinghy: "I imagine grieving is like being in a small dinghy anchored to shore. There is extra rope in the dinghy – sometimes the person in the dinghy goes out as far as they can, sometimes the people on shore pull them back a little just to make sure they are safe. The rope line is strong – if the water gets too rough, numerous people on shore start reeling the dinghy in; at other times, the dinghy remains afloat, and the person is alone for days, as that is what they feel they need. The horizon is always being watched and examined so if the weather changes, the dinghy will be rolled in quickly. At some moments, the water is clear, smooth, reflective, and at other moments it is a frenzy of pain and emotion. The line is sturdy, though, and remains tied to the shore. The person in the dinghy just has to give the signal and someone is waiting." Hope is the trust that no matter what happens, we will be carried, supported, even when we cannot ask for help.

Hope. Elusive. Transformative. Part of our wiring as Christians. Thank God.

Mariette Martineau is an author, wife and mother, and the Canadian Religious Stewardship Community Consultant for three religious communities in Saskatoon. She is the former Religious Education and Family Life Coordinator of the Kenora Catholic District School Board.

God Holds Death and Life

Donald Bolen

The challenge is laid out in the clearest of ways in 1 Peter 3:15: "always be ready to give an account of the hope that is within you." We live at a time when many find hope to be elusive, hard to find, hard to hold onto. I doubt that it was ever easy to be a person of hope, and it is certainly not easy in our complex and wounded world.

I grew up being taught and coming to believe, at first in the simplest ways, that God holds death and life, that death doesn't have the last word. From the time I was seven and experienced my father's death from cancer, I was encouraged by my family and by our church community to trust that though he was gone – with all the finality that death brings – he was also somehow alive in God and that through God our relationship with him was not fully severed. I have been on what you might call a paschal quest ever since, looking for a narrative that is vast enough to hold our beginnings and endings and all that lies between and beyond them, with hope. My Christian faith is a searching faith, with a restlessness that has never fully settled, but I have found a home there, paraphrasing St. Augustine, to seek in order to find in order to seek still more. And trusting that the deeper narrative is that God in Christ has come in search of us.

A series of quotes that I have held onto over the years communicate a deeply attractive hope-filled perspective on human life: among them, Julian of Norwich's "All shall be well, and all manner of things shall be well" and "Everything is going to be fine in the end. If it's not fine, it's not the end" (attributed to Oscar Wilde, among others). But these very encouraging words need to be balanced with some of the harshness and incompleteness that we encounter in the human condition.

I *want* to say – in as definitive a way as I can – that I love this human life, despite all of its challenges and frustrations, and that ultimately I trust it because God is in it, holding all the frayed and tattered ends together in a fabric whose beauty will one day be visible to us. I want to share with others in homilies and talks and in my daily living that life is beautiful, sacred and trustworthy, echoing the inspiring words of Rabbi

Abraham Heschel that "just to be is a blessing, just to live is holy." But to be a bearer of hope in a way that can withstand the strong winds of critical thinking and skepticism in our culture requires that we also grapple with what novelist Graham Greene called "life at its dirty work."

Human life on earth, marked by countless gifts which bring meaning and joy to our lives, is also marked by decay, discord and death. There is a great deal of suffering in our world, not all of it caused by human immaturity and sin. When sudden illness takes the life of someone who was deeply alive, depriving people of life or of love and happiness long sought after; when communities and nations who through their history have struggled and experienced injustice continue to collide with each other, leading to conflicts that seem intractable; when life seems to ask more than we can give; when human brokenness leads to a hunger for and abuse of power which in turn hurts and terrorizes others; when in a thousand different ways we as individuals and as communities find it difficult or impossible to live well and meaningfully together, hope can seem to reside at a distant and receding horizon.

The created order, and the human condition as we

know it, clothed with strands of beauty and harshness interwoven, spin into questions resonating throughout human history: How does it all hold together? What is going on here? There is too much grace, too much wonder, to give in easily to a despair that says it is all meaningless. There is too much brokenness, too much suffering, to have a facile hope that all is well when it is clearly not.

So, when I am asked where I find hope, in the first instance I am looking for a hope that can somehow take account of the full breadth of our experience, holding the human venture within a broader narrative that can at least make some sense of the way things are.

When I have the privilege and opportunity to confirm young people, I try to share the heart and foundation of Christian hope in the simplest of terms: that God, author of all creation and of ourselves, loves us with a boundless love; that God is always trying to speak with us through the created world and at the depths of our lives; that out of love, God chooses to enter into our broken world, the eternal Word taking flesh in order to be where we are, to speak love in a way that we can more fully see and receive it; that in the life of Jesus, we see God's face, and it is a face of mercy and compassion, communicating a desire that we might be transformed by that love and share it with others; that in his death, Jesus reveals to us that God's love knows no bounds; that in his resurrection, God has the last word, bringing life from death, forgiving us for the worst possible thing we could do and promising us a future full of hope; that in sending the Holy Spirit, God accompanies us every step of this earthly life, strengthening us to walk as disciples of the crucified and risen Lord.

There are no doubt better ways to paint the big picture of who God is and what God is doing for us, but I am convinced that sharing the big picture of what gives us hope opens the door to finding hope in a second litany, the litany of even the smallest and most everyday things: the first glimpse of the sun bending over the horizon with each new day; every new birth; each life-giving encounter with another; the experience of forgiveness; the grace, after struggle and failures, to try again and again; the song of the meadowlark the first time you hear it in the spring; the smell of lilacs in May and clover in the heat of the summer; the life that is given us at each moment, awakening chords of deep joy within.

And so, despite all the frustrations, injustices and contradictions of this life, and daily buoyed by its wonders and beauty, I carry a deep gratitude within me, and seek to share that gratitude with others.

> *Thanks to the human heart by which we live,*
> *Thanks to its tenderness, its joys, and fears,*
> *To me the meanest flower that blows can give*
> *Thoughts that do often lie too deep for tears.*
>
> William Wordsworth,
> "Intimations of Immortality from
> Recollections of Early Childhood"

Christian hope leads to gratitude, but it also leads to resilience, courage and action. Hope is not an end in itself. May our hope inspire lives of commitment, generosity and trust as we spend ourselves at the service of others and our world, echoing the great self-gift of God in our crucified and Risen Lord.

Donald Bolen currently serves as the Catholic Archbishop of Regina, Saskatchewan. He has spent much of his priestly and episcopal life working on ecumenical and justice issues.

An Unwavering Spark

Stefany Dupont

There is beauty in the diversity of languages our world holds. I say this because as a francophone, when I think of hope, I think of the word *espérance*, which differs from *espoir*, despite having the same root. *Espoir* is the direct translation of the word "hope" in English, but *espérance* goes deeper, suggesting a sustained, evergreen faith in a larger-than-life, spiritual happy ending. As far back as I can remember, I have had the privilege of living with that kind of hope, and I'm convinced it is what has helped me survive the most life-threatening, challenging moments of my life.

For a while now, I have thought of this *espérance* as an unwavering spark within me. Its existence is an immense, beautiful mystery that cannot be explained rationally. I just know it to be there, never faltering. It whispers to me that despite the difficulties I may be facing, despite the catastrophic, horrendous events happening in our world, there is reason to believe and fight for all the beauty, wonder and love it contains. Its instinctive melody sings to me that there is an explanation, a cause, a structure to the chaos that life can be.

I remember the spark manifesting itself when I was around age 10 and our English teacher told us about the idea of people ending their lives voluntarily to stop their suffering. I did not understand the complexity of this concept back then and fervently raised my hand to insist that such a thing should never be done because there could always, always be a possibility of healing within this life. While I do hold a much more nuanced position today, this act of immediately standing up for the possibility of better days as a child reminds me how long something within me has fostered the belief that the future would eventually align with everything that makes life worth living. I still know it to be true, but I understand that it might not be within this life or within my limited human perception of existence. Because yes, even if it is not given to us now, how could the answer to all our doubts not be one of beauty when each day, we discover a bit more about the complexity of matter, the perfection of music, the infiniteness of mathematics, the power of nature?

I can say, though, that I might not have witnessed this spark of hope, let alone have it transform into a flame or fire, without other, more tangible elements in my life that allowed it to manifest itself to me. This spark grows and lives because of the deep love and care I receive daily from my family and the friends I have made over the years. It blossomed slowly thanks to my mother introducing my brother and me early on to the teachings of someone named Jesus, despite our protests and disruptive behaviour in the church pews. Its flame burns when I have the chance to walk in nature and witness the colours of the flowers and trees around me. It dances when, on a difficult day, despite frustration and tiredness, I find myself smiling when a child glances curiously in my direction, their eyes twinkling with wonder. Indeed, it is facilitated in the first place due to the first few levels of Abraham Maslow's hierarchy of needs pyramid having almost always been fulfilled in my life – I have never known war or famine, discrimination or catastrophe. I come from a well-off family. When I became severely ill at age 13, and within each new period causing my health to be fragile with varying intensity, I was supported by an incredible team of nurses, pharmacists, therapists, doctors and volunteers. And I could always count on the miracles done by Jesus, whose story, really, is the very definition of hope. The luck of the draw has made it so that I never felt completely alone and have always had access to the plus side of the equation.

I recognize that this foundation creates the right environment for the spark to evolve. And yet, this spark has been nourished in me by witnessing other individuals undoubtedly riding along its power without having the privilege of such solid security nets. Whether it be a leader like Nelson Mandela, a family of refugees rebuilding their life after forcible displacement, a generous saint like Mother Teresa, or the parents of my friend Jen who died at age 40, the knowledge that such endurance and conviction is possible despite severe, sustained, human-made, forcibly unjust hardship propagates itself to energize the spark of hope within me. I believe it is this ability to harness that sparkle, that glow, that ultimately allows resilience to emerge.

Like I said, I am no Nelson Mandela. Yet, there came a point in my life where I stopped second-guessing people repeating to me that I was "brave" for facing my illness. I thought it a dull refrain because I did not feel brave – instead, I felt I simply did not have a choice, and I had to go along with the situation. Yet, when I look back at the hours of physiotherapy I had to do when I lost all mobility, at the countless days spent in therapy, at the number of sick friends I lost over the years, at the gritted teeth through procedures and needles, at the weight lost and gained, at the repeated home workouts to ensure I rebuilt my strength only to shed it again, I start to see that I also possess innate qualities that fed my spark. This *espérance* might have always been there, but it could have diminished to a sliver of dim, passing light. Sometimes, it was at risk, but it was never fully compromised because there was always a reason to bring it back to life. That is why I try to do my best to ensure that my fire lights the fire of others around me, as people did for me. Because fire can do just that: spread.

Stefany Dupont is originally from Gatineau, Québec. She now lives in Vancouver, where she is pursuing a teaching degree.

Storying Our Hope

STEPHEN BEDE SCHARPER

"For me, hope is embedded in our stories..."

Anishinaabe artist Chief Lady Bird,
Rama First Nation

THE ABOVE INSIGHT accompanies Chief Lady Bird's stunning mural, *Bgosendmowih (Hope)*, which graces the historic Leuty Boathouse in Toronto, Canada's, east end.

This suggests to me that hope needs to take a form, whether in our dreams, in our aspirations or in the stories we tell.

In keeping with this understanding, here are four personal stories that speak to the wellsprings of my own hope.

Grandma "Mirth"

My grandma loved to "cut up."

This involved a frolicsome exchange of stories, shared memories, joy and laughter. *Lots* of laughter. Consequently, my father dubbed my mom's mom "Mirth." The name fit.

I have a vivid memory of my grandma, enveloped in knee-slapping laughter, removing her glasses to wipe away tears as all of us were caught in her contagious delight.

But these were no Pollyannish tears. My grandma had passed through many hard spaces in her lifetime.

She was a young woman during World War I, witnessing many of her friends march off to the mustard-gassed trenches of that ghastly conflict.

As a working mother of three, she endured devastating financial hardship during the Great Depression, married to a caring but alcoholic husband. During World War II, her 17-year-old son, lying about his age, joined the U.S. Marines and was shipped off to the savagery of the South Pacific theatre.

She endured the ambient anxiety of the Cold War, the political and cultural upheaval of the 1960s, and the growing gap between the haves and have-nots inaugurated by the Thatcher-Reagan-Mulroney "greed-is-good" era.

Yet, through it all, it was her joy that served as her indelible trademark, a joy sustained by a rock-ribbed faith.

"Never underestimate the power of positive thinking," she would urge us, "or the power of prayer." And whenever we faced our own challenges, she would instruct us to "always trust in the Holy Spirit."

In heeding her own words, her nearly century-long life became a graced space where hope and joy embraced – and "cut up."

Jane Goodall and a Graduation "Hoo-Hoo"-tenanny

Convocation Hall, University of Toronto, spring 2009. I had just finished reading the citation for Dr. Jane Goodall, the famed primatologist, who was being awarded an honorary doctorate for her pioneering scientific and conservation work in Tanzania and beyond. I was about to sit down when Jane called me back to the front of the stage.

"Stephen," she said. "I want to thank you on behalf of the chimpanzees."

"And in the way the chimpanzees would," she added with an impish smile.

Arching her arms around my shoulders without touching them, she instructed me to do the same to her. "This is not a spectator sport," she laughed. "This is how the chimpanzees would thank you." She quickly began to move her arms back and forth in a pincer movement, uttering with increasing volume, "Hoo Hoo Hoo Hoo HOO HOO HOO," and invited me to echo her.

This was done in full academic regalia, on film, in front of the university chancellor, president, provost, dozens of faculty, the 500-plus members of the graduating class and their assorted guests.

As the simian "Hoo Hoo Hoo HOOs" began to crescendo, so did the laughter from the audience, bouncing off the august domed roof of Convocation Hall and encircling us all.

It was Jane Goodall in frolicsome splendour, enlivening our campus with her ebullient spirit. Though she had been on the front lines of unspeakable animal cruelty and had witnessed first-hand the ravages of climate change in Africa and other parts of the global South, her sense of hope and humour were intact, and riotously infectious. She, too, knew how to "cut up."

Prize Tomato

"This whole class, I've been trying to see the connection between the environment and social justice."

Fernando, a student in my environment course at the

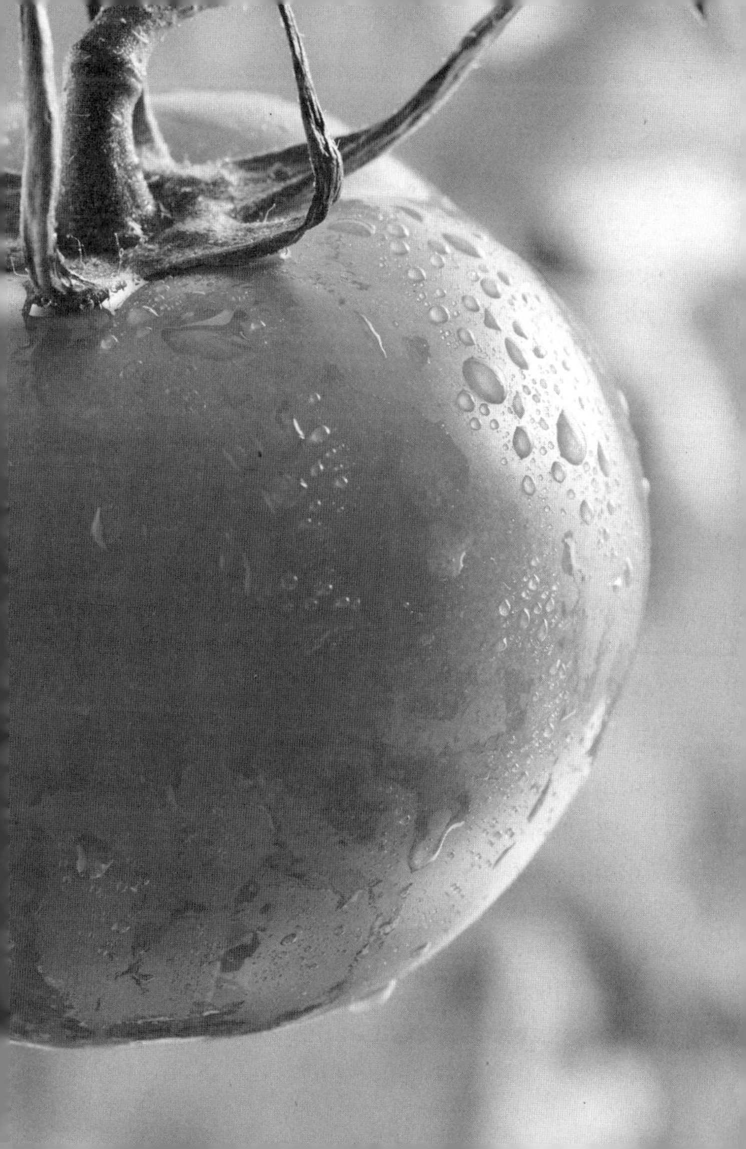

University of Notre Dame, shared this during his oral exam. He had completed an immersion experience with an urban agricultural group for at-risk youth; he was now trying to relate his field experience to the course material.

He had been working with Alfonso, age 10, whose brother had already entered a gang. The hope was that Alfonso would follow another path.

Through a community garden, Alfonso had raised an award-winning tomato. "When I saw Alfonso's beaming face as he received the award, and sensed the pride and joy he had in this tomato, it clicked," Fernando recounted. "I finally saw the connection between ecology and social justice."

A connection of hope and joy.

The D-Day Beaches of Normandy

During a recent research junket to England, my wife Hilary presented me with an unexpected 40th wedding anniversary gift. "We're going to Normandy," she declared. "I've made all the arrangements."

It was a wonderful surprise. Ever since watching Robert Mitchum in *The Longest Day* as an eight-year-old kid sprawled in front of our Zenith TV set, I had wanted to visit the D-Day beaches. And now we were going. (Given the current threats to democracy unfolding in the U.S., with parallels to the rise of fascism in Nazi Germany, the visit seemed particularly timely.)

After touring the stirring Juno Beach Centre and the solemn rows of graves at Omaha Beach's Normandy American Cemetery, Hilary asked me how I felt.

I replied that I felt surprisingly centred and quietly hopeful.

A novelist and anthropologist, she responded that she had felt the same, and she shared with me the following reflection:

I have found a centeredness here—walking with the water.

I expected to find all the strange and difficult traumas of place-harm: the tragedies and horrors of the war strewn across the long, seemingly endless stretches of beach. All the blood spilled here... every grain of sand stained... the very foam of the waves forever tinged... the wind itself a restless and anguished captive to memories of unimaginable suffering.

No doubt all that trauma is here. I was afraid of it;

fearful of being wounded by coming too close.

Yet, walking with the water – listening – it struck me that there are many kinds of presences who might be here, not just the disturbed ones.

There is a wisdom here, too – the steady singing of the waves, hoarse today, yesterday sweetly hushed. A wisdom which has faced the horrors and bravely grieves. A wisdom which eschews forgetfulness as a solution and yet will not surrender joy, or beauty, or mystery; will not give up mirth and mischief – even danger – to trauma. Somehow the beaches, the water, wind and sky have moved on. They have kept faith with God and steadfastly honour the dead. It is sobering and yet healing to be here. As if place-harm can yield a quiet, persistent courage – turning rock into stone; stone into pebbles; pebbles into sand –

As if there is no final "put out the light." God would never say it.

A mirthful grandmother, an inspired primatologist, a prideful urban gardener, a steadfast coastline...

These stories, as Chief Lady Bird observes, "embed" hope. It is also my belief that they can engender hope in their telling.

Stephen Bede Scharper explores the interweaving of ecology, spirituality, justice and compassion at the University of Toronto and beyond.

Sustaining Sources of Hope

CHRISTINE WAY SKINNER

IT CAN BE a challenge to be hopeful, at times. Half an hour of listening to the news will remind us that the planet is facing an environmental crisis, that human blood is being shed in dozens of wars across the globe, that we have failed to end poverty despite our substantial technological capability, and that even our beloved Church has been exposed as scandalously sinful. A backward glance at history will tell us that, while the particulars may vary, humankind has always faced fear-provoking conditions. Matthew's Gospel encourages us, however, by reminding us that these events are not the end of the story. Jesus says, "you will hear of wars and rumours of wars; *see that you are not alarmed*; for this must take place, but the end is not yet. For nation will rise against nation, and kingdom against kingdom, and there will be famines and earthquakes in various places: all this is but the beginning of the birth pangs" (Matthew 24:6-8). Something new, something better is always being born.

So, where do we find firm footing on which to base our hopefulness? Certainly not in denial. That just makes us part of the problem. Our Christian call is to be midwives to the new and better that is being born. But in the thick of struggle, we also need encouragement, support and sustenance. I have always found these to be provided in stories of healing, personal victory and growth – stories that remind me that God is more powerful than any force of evil in this world. And where can such stories be found? In sacred Scripture, in history and in our very own lives.

Stories of Scripture

There is virtually no experience of hardship in life for which we cannot find a story in Scripture that seems to be written specifically to tell us we are not alone. When we experience the infidelity of friends, we can look to the story of Peter's betrayal of Jesus, where we are guided to hope that understanding, forgiveness and conversion are all within reach. If the betrayals are familial, there is a large selection. The tales of Joseph and his brothers and of David and Bathsheba teach us that the incredible pain and destruction that come with familial betrayal are not the end of the story. If we find ourselves to be the victims of unjust authorities, we can look to Susanna, Daniel, Paul and, of course, Jesus himself. If we grieve the loss of our homeland, we can weep by the rivers of Babylon with the Israelites, and if we grieve the loss of our loved one, we can place before our minds the image of Mary holding her beloved Son in her arms after he was removed from the cross. The knowledge that God brings people home from exile and that God raises Jesus from the dead can give us hope that we, too, will be brought home and will rise from destruction. And, finally, we can discover nearly every hardship imaginable in the story of Job. Despite his suffering, Job was able to remain faithful and hopeful and even to declare in his torment, "Blessed be the name of the Lord!"

These stories manifest the triumph of God's plan for salvation over all obstacles, including human sinfulness. They also caution patience and faithfulness, for sometimes it takes generations for God's promises to be realized. Some biblical characters never see their hopes realized in their lifetime. Abraham and Sarah, for instance, did not witness the lives of their descendants as numerous as the stars. Not all God's promises are meant to be fulfilled before our eyes, it seems.

Nevertheless, our hope-filled fidelity is meant to contribute to God's plan for humankind.

Stories of History

Studying history can also be a source of hope. Knowledge of history affords us a long view: we can observe that the tyrants of history never get the last word. They do great damage, it is true, but they never win in any ultimate fashion. God and goodness ever triumph. Joan of Arc is remembered by almost everyone; the bishop who was responsible for her death is known by few. Gandhi's example inspires millions. The names of the oppressing government officials against whom he protested have faded into historical oblivion. We can read about saints and heroic people from all religious traditions who have sacrificed their comfort to help the most vulnerable in the world and have changed things for the better for all who followed. We can look to virtuous people who engaged in heroic acts of love and kindness amid the evil of the Holocaust. We can see encouraging examples of humankind learning from such experiences and striving to defeat the systems that allowed tyrants to emerge. Though it is true that we have not yet learned to live in peace and that we do not yet have a just world, we have, I believe, moved forward. Few cultures now believe that it is permissible to perpetrate violence against children and women. As nations, we are united in declaring that people have rights not only to food, water and shelter but also to get an education, to have liberty of religion and conscience, to move about freely, to select their leaders and to experience leisure. While human progress over the ages may not always be straightforward, it does seem to be the case that the long arc of history bends toward justice.[1]

Stories of Our Lives

Finally, but just as importantly, we can reach back in our own personal histories to discover reasons to hope. We can recall times when we felt soundly defeated, only to experience the hands of good Samaritans pulling us out of the mud and holding us as we walked a little further down the road to stability. We can remember instances when we encountered personal difficulty only to be able to see later that they yielded great good

---

[1] From a sermon preached by civil rights leader Rev. Theodore Parker in 1853 and popularized by Martin Luther King, Jr.

for someone else in our community. And we can recollect moments when we were able to achieve peace, reconciliation, kindness or self-giving love when the odds were against us.

In these stories from Scripture, history and our own lives, we find evidence for Julian of Norwich's assurance that in the end, "all shall be well." In these stories, God bestows rich resources to assist us in "hoping against hope" (Romans 4:18).

Christine Way Skinner is a doctoral candidate in theology at Regis St. Michael's in Toronto. She has been a lay ecclesial minister for over 30 years.

The Hand of God

CONSTANCE PRICE

Two manifestations of the love of God for us give me great hope: the good and selfless acts of others that emerge in times of loss, and the Church's teachings that we, as the People of God, are on a journey that does not end here. The first takes what God has planted in us and shows what we are meant to do and to be for others. The second shows that we are never alone. We are always accompanied by others as we walk together on the Christian journey.

The Good that Blossoms in Times of Crisis

Twenty-nine years ago, one man's anger exploded in an act of domestic terrorism in the United States. One hundred and sixty-eight people were killed in the bombing of the Alfred P. Murrah federal building in Oklahoma City. Nineteen of the dead were children, most of whom were attending a daycare centre in the building. The national memorial service was heart-wrenching. Some of the parents of the murdered children clutched teddy bears and stared vacantly, their faces marked with grief. By contrast, my two-year-old nephew, whom I was babysitting, slept peacefully on my lap as I tearfully watched and prayed.

After the service, there was a televised panel discussion with several religious leaders. The interviewer asked the leaders how and where one could possibly find God in the midst of such tragedy, trauma and grief. The rabbi on the panel responded that we see God in the goodness of the people who helped those affected by the loss and pain, from the first responders to the individual acts of assistance and comfort. His comment struck a chord in me; I found myself thinking about it as remarkable stories of good works and charitable acts toward survivors and the bereaved emerged in the weeks that followed. Somehow, good did seem to blossom where there is crisis or trauma. And the face of God became more visible through the witness and works of people as they helped one another.

A cynic might say that something is wrong if the love and presence of God through the goodness of others emerges only when there is trauma or crisis. Surely the world would be a better place if such acts of charity happened more often? Of course! But the lesson in it for me is that God has planted in each of us the ability to do good in service to others and act with a compassionate heart. As a reminder, I created a playlist that contains videos of heartfelt tributes to some of our social and Church leaders who have gone the distance in setting up ways to help others by outreach in justice and love. It also has events showing stars of the music world voluntarily sharing their talents to raise funds and support for others whose circumstances are dire. Finally, a few videos show the creative use of musicians' interpretation of pieces that they performed for the composers in an act of tribute and appreciation for the gifts of the other. I play my 'feel-good' list regularly. I am energized by the gratefulness and giving of others and by the good deeds done to help those who are in crisis. As the rabbi had pointed out after the Oklahoma City bombing, loss and trauma often are occasions for the best to come out in others as they work to alleviate or reduce suffering. The impetus to do good and to walk with others is something that is within us, given to us by God. And this gives me hope!

We Are Never Alone

Since that week in 1995, I have had many opportunities to test the rabbi's theory in my own life (of course, I am not equating the violent deaths of 168 people and the massive injuries others suffered to my personal experiences). The litany of my losses and trauma begins here – losing almost all of my close friends and family to death and disease; losing much of my eyesight for five weeks before being diagnosed with multiple sclerosis (MS); losing my ability to walk or work out at the gym after a medical mistake; losing my sense of security after an assault by a stranger and, years later, a stalker; or the emotional, physical, financial and spiritual trauma that goes with 12 years of long-distance caregiving while trying to complete a doctorate and cope with MS symptoms and piecing together three part-time jobs. It does not, however, end with sadness or a desire for pity.

As I reflect upon my losses, the first mental image that arises – sort of a free association – is not the image of the trauma but the image of someone or some community that came to my rescue with good words, prayers, works and sometimes with concrete help, like respite care when I was caregiving, or the consolation offered by the police at the time of my assault; the stranger who asked if he could keep his hand between my head and the rock it was resting on when I fell and had a concussion; paramedics who have literally picked me up from the floor; the anonymous monetary gift that was given to me 42 years ago when I was a 20-year-old student, far from home, with a new diagnosis of MS; the parish that gave me a bursary so I could keep going with my studies in a new country.

With such accompaniment and goodness, I feel the hand of God on my shoulder. I picture myself walking on a wide road with the people who have taught me about the love of Christ and his walk with us, entering into my walk, my journey, my own pilgrimage. The people on the road with me are both friends and loved ones who have passed from this world as well as people who are currently in my life. I can't see where we are going, but I know that we are moving. Together. On a pilgrimage that is the gift of my life from God. The Church teaches about our earthly pilgrimage toward the heavenly Jerusalem. This must be a part of that journey where death and suffering does not have the last word. We are not alone. We walk with others, witness to others and accompany others. We see a glimpse of God when we truly walk with others and let them walk with us. Christ is with us, and we are not alone. In this I find great hope.

Dr. Constance Price works in theological and pastoral education. She is the author of Beyond the Ramp: A Parish Guide to Welcoming Persons with Disabilities *(Novalis and Twenty-Third Publications, 2020).*

Social Movements, Fountains of Social Hope

Joe Gunn

You've heard the question raised a thousand times... usually at the end of a guest speaker's presentation on some pressing social issue. You've come to expect it, like the long-awaited crescendo concluding any meaningful event. You're able to let out a sigh of relief when that most infamous of questions has finally been spoken:

"So, where do *you* find hope?"

Now, of course there is nothing wrong with searching for hope. After all, isn't it one of the three theological virtues of Christian faith? Like you, gentle reader, I want to discover what hope we are worthy of in this time and space. But since there are so many kinds of hope, what I "hope" to offer is quite specific: How might we be able to understand and engender *social hope* today?

Why focus on *social hope*? Simply because it would be too small an enterprise to only attempt to capture meaningful hope for myself. With so many needs and injustices present in this world, with Creation crying out for protection and healing, religions and spiritualities must be directed outward. As Pope Francis repeatedly says in one of his most challenging (and least understood) statements, "No one can be saved alone." Social hope has become an expansive moral imperative today.

Context is so very important whenever we consider such weighty questions. Here in North America, we live in the richest society ever known in human history. Can hope be the same thing for us here in the privileged North as for a woman and her children living in a refugee camp? Such a comparison stretches the imagination! Their context of struggling for daily survival is a lived reality for many of the planet's 35 million refugees today. When I worked in refugee camps in Central America, hope was framed as security for families from violence and hunger, a modicum of health care and, on the horizon, the possibility of eventual return to hopefully unchanged village communities that had once known peace. The verb "to hope" in Spanish is *esperar* – it also means "to wait." We North Americans are not Latino romantic idealists – waiting is not our strong suit! We want solutions to be available and immediate. Long-term commitments (or even long-term commitments to social struggle) are rarely considered feasible or desirable. Mainstream Canadian society insidiously conditions us all to comfortable, bourgeois values, lifestyles and practices – which invariably have infected our faith traditions. Perhaps we've even domesticated our definitions of social hope.

Vandana Shiva (an Indian scholar and environmentalist) once wrote that "the context is not in your control, but your commitment is yours to make." Therefore, social hope must be lived as a verb.

Maybe asking others where to find hope is not the most pressing question. Maybe we should be asking ourselves, "Where today should I find *the social courage* to act?"

Today, in the context of social and economic justice ministry in Canada, hope deserves a bigger frame than is offered by traditional institutions. Rather than dismissing social hope, we must turn to discover it in new guises, with new actors, in new forms – discovering it by acting. In my recent experience, social hope is now to be found in (both religious and secular) movements for change.

So, let's get specific: What are a couple of social movements that can enlarge social hope for Canadian faith communities today?

One very new organization calls itself the Office of Religious Congregations for Integral Ecology (ORCIE). Understanding the frame of "integral ecology" found in Pope Francis's 2015 encyclical *Laudato Si'* as hearing the cry of the poor and the cry of the Earth, over two dozen religious congregations are attempting to weave together the energies of their various charisms to create greater impact for systemic change. After reflecting on the call to ecological conversion, congregations discerned that many local initiatives have been undertaken (in greening properties, planting gardens, preserving nature, etc.) and carrying out educational activities. But gaps were identified in necessary collaborative advocacy, such as on the pressing climate crisis. So, ORCIE's mission is to "enhance the capacity of Catholic religious congregations to collaboratively increase their impact on policy change towards social and economic justice at the level of the Canadian federal government, at international levels and before large corporate business entities." ORCIE members have twice travelled to Parliament Hill to meet members of Parliament and lobby all five Canadian political parties. At a recent meeting, a seasoned Assistant Deputy Minister remarked that he agreed to meet with ORCIE because in all his years of service, he had never met representatives of faith communities who were interested in federal policy concerns!

Other remarkable work is being accomplished by the Mouvement Laudato Si' Movement (LSM) – Canada. Part of the global Catholic response to the environmental crisis, LSM – Canada has produced a "Catholic Eco-Investment Accelerator Toolkit" that allows individuals and organizations to move their financial holdings to green impact investing. Already, my parish and the university where I work have divested from fossil fuels in their financial portfolios. LSM – Canada's campaign for 2024 has a greater, longer-term goal: inviting Catholics to write to their local bishop, asking him to divest all diocesan finances.

My friend Maude Barlow writes in her 2022 book, *Still Hopeful: Lessons from a Lifetime of Activism*, that our efforts are not really about achieving a goal. Maude's activism is all about "building movements and finding like-minded people to carry the load with you."

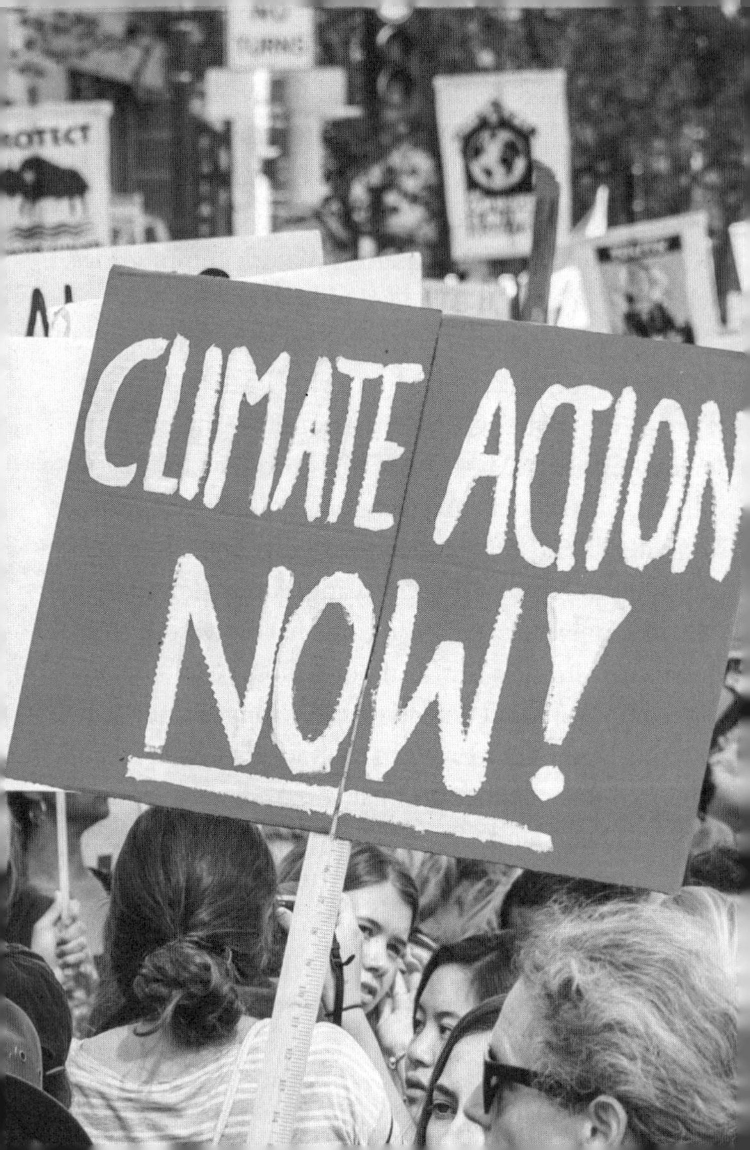
CLIMATE ACTION
NOW!

A final story... Some years ago, our faith-based organizations were promoting action on the Truth and Reconciliation Commission of Canada's 94 Calls to Action. We organized a webinar where over 1,000 participants listened to the three Commissioners: Murray Sinclair, Willie Littlechild and Marie Wilson. When asked if there was really any hope of success in such a historic endeavour, Marie responded by reminding us that the reason we persevere in actions for justice is because, ultimately, we ourselves are changed.

This is a profound theological insight. We discover social hope, lived through our action in the world, through social movements for justice – and live ourselves and the world into conversion and change.

Joe Gunn is the former executive director of Citizens for Public Justice. He is a speaker, activist and author on social and environmental concerns.

"That's Why You Were Baptized"
The Decision to Hope

Anne Walsh

A FEW YEARS ago, I was given a diagnosis of cancer. My first response was to be paralyzed, shocked, afraid and unable to process what was happening to me. I heard the words my doctor was saying, but they did not sink in, and I left her office in a fog. A friend of mine serves as a chaplain in the same hospital, and my feet made their way to his office, almost of their own volition. My body had made a decision that pointed me toward hope long before my conscious mind was aware of what was happening.

In his office, in his calm presence, I was able to take a step back and begin to feel the shock, grief and fear that were my initial response to the words that had washed over me. I began to comprehend, and with that comprehension I began to feel a resolve. That resolve welled up from a place deep within, and words from another friend in another time and place came back to me. In that instance, facing another medical crisis and feeling paralyzed, I had confessed to a friend, "I can't pray." His response surprised me: "That's okay. That's why you were baptized. You were baptized so that, in times like this, the rest of us would pray for you."

Those words had touched me deeply, and they changed the way I looked at things, particularly my own illness. My friend's words moved me to a decision – a fundamental decision to hope. Now, as if those words had been deposits in a bank account from which I could make withdrawals anytime I liked, the words came back to me with renewed force. I decided that I was more than my diagnosis. I was not "cancer," and I was not "struggling with" cancer. I decided that I would live to the full. I made a few very practical decisions. I decided to hope, and hope is the most practical of virtues.

What did hope look like? I decided that I would be no doctor's worst patient. I decided that, even though I was living with a serious illness, I still had the power and ability to reach out and help others. I decided that I was not and would not be a victim.

Once again, the power of that fundamental decision took hold. I realized that how I am going to "be" does not depend on whether I "beat it." Success is not a result but an attitude, rooted in hope.

Renewing my decision to hope changed everything. On my journey through surgery, radiation and follow-up, I met the most wonderful people; I walked with them, and they with me. My changed perspective allowed me to see the skilled hands of oncologists, surgeons, nurses, radiologists and radiation technicians as the healing hands of Jesus. That changed perspective also allowed me to comfort and calm the oncologist who was having difficulty getting the biopsy sample that was at one point required, and it allowed me to help a radiation technician process some of his anger and disillusionment at the Church, which I in some way represented for him.

Hope truly is the most practical of virtues. It is more than an attitude and more than optimism. Having hope means that I determine what is good and worth working for, and then take concrete steps and engage in concrete actions that build hope, breathe life into it, and bring it more and more fully into being. Hope draws on and builds courage. Hope draws on and builds compassion, mercy and resilience of spirit. On some days more than others, hope seems elusive, and that's where the decision to hope comes into play. On those days when I do not feel as hopeful, I call on that bank reserve of the fundamental decision that I made: I keep on putting one foot in front of the other, looking for ways to exercise hope, live hope, *be* hope. And I am not alone. The knowledge instilled in me – that baptism assures me that on the days when I feel my reserve of hope is pretty shallow, others are praying for me – gives me courage to go on. It gives me the compassion to pray for others.

The words of the Czech poet, activist and statesman Vaclav Havel ring true for me:

> Hope is not the same thing as optimism. It is not the conviction that something will turn out well, but the certainty that something makes sense, regardless of how it turns out. In short, I think that the deepest and most important form of hope, the only one that can keep us above water and urge us to good works, and the only true source of the breathtaking dimension of the human spirit and its efforts, is something we get, as it were, from 'elsewhere.' It is also this hope, above all, that gives us the strength to live and continually to try new

things, even in conditions that seem as hopeless as ours do, here and now.[2]

What makes sense for me, having faced significant illness, is that hope is a fundamental decision that I must make, that we all must make. Having made that decision in the fundamental sense, I then must make it again every day, in every situation. Hope is really drawing on the practical power of the Resurrection of Jesus Christ, made manifest every day in our lives, propelling us from fear to hope, from darkness to light, from apathy to love, from pain to healing. Hope is what empowers us to keep putting one foot in front of the other.

Anne Walsh is from St. John's, Newfoundland and Labrador. She works with the Redemptorists in Adult Faith Formation and coordinating and resourcing Partnership in Mission. She holds the Office of Partnership in Mission for the Redemptorists worldwide and is Chair of the Redemptorist General Commission for Partnership in Mission.

---

[2] Vaclav Havel, "The kind of hope I often think about," in *Disturbing the Peace: A Conversation with Karel Hvizdala*, trans and intro. by Paul Wilson (New York: Vintage Books, 1990), 181. In Rebecca Solnit, *Hope in the Dark: Untold Histories, Wild Possibilities* (Chicago: Haymarket Books, 2016).

Rejoice in hope,
be patient in suffering,
persevere in prayer.

Romans 12:12